My Life's Reflection: A Life Review Workbook, by Samantha A. Bechtel and Alicia M. Bogard, provides a clear path for individuals to document the significant aspects of their life's journey. The first section of this book focuses on critical milestones, transitions, and life events as well as deeper personal reflections of our values, spirituality, and hopes. The outcome of sharing these reflections will be a cherished gift for future generations. The second section of this book sensitively and comprehensively tackles the often difficult-to-talk-about topics of grief and personal loss. With the authors applying their years of personal experience to these subjects, the reader will appreciate the practical information and insights that directly address grief and loss as well as how to capture the important elements of a life review.

—Barry K. Baines, MD,
Hospice Medical Director
and author of *Ethical Wills: Putting Your Values on Paper*

In the many years I have worked for hospice, I have looked for a book such as this that allows someone to give the gift of truly knowing you. This book provides a threefold benefit. First, it serves to help someone relive memories that include frivolous as well as sacred events that can trigger conversations that lead to healing. Second, it allows family and friends the opportunity to "fill in the gaps" that were never known about someone we love. Lastly, the contents of this book can help to bring continuity to future generations who will now know why they special ordered that orange phone. This is a wonderful, useful tool for everyone.

—Jan W. Bucholz, MSN, MBA, RN, CHC

My Life's REFLECTION
A LIFE REVIEW WORKBOOK

My Life's REFLECTION
A LIFE REVIEW WORKBOOK

SAMANTHA A. BECHTEL MSSA, LISW
AND ALICIA M. BOGARD MSW, LISW

TATE PUBLISHING
AND ENTERPRISES, LLC

My Life's Reflection
Copyright © 2012 by Samantha A. Bechtel MSSA, LISW and Alicia M. Bogard MSW, LISW. All rights reserved.

No part of this publication may be reproduced, stored in a retrieval system or transmitted in any way by any means, electronic, mechanical, photocopy, recording or otherwise without the prior permission of the author except as provided by USA copyright law.

This book is designed to provide accurate and authoritative information with regard to the subject matter covered. This information is given with the understanding that neither the author nor Tate Publishing, LLC is engaged in rendering legal, professional advice. Since the details of your situation are fact dependent, you should additionally seek the services of a competent professional.

The opinions expressed by the author are not necessarily those of Tate Publishing, LLC.

Published by Tate Publishing & Enterprises, LLC
127 E. Trade Center Terrace | Mustang, Oklahoma 73064 USA
1.888.361.9473 | www.tatepublishing.com

Tate Publishing is committed to excellence in the publishing industry. The company reflects the philosophy established by the founders, based on Psalm 68:11,
"The Lord gave the word and great was the company of those who published it."

Book design copyright © 2012 by Tate Publishing, LLC. All rights reserved.
Cover design by Nicole McDaniel
Interior design by Nathan Harmony

Published in the United States of America

ISBN: 978-1-62147-233-9
1. Social Science / Death & Dying
2. Self-Help / Death, Grief, Bereavement
12.09.20

Dedication

This book is dedicated with love to *you*.

Acknowledgments

We wish to thank Stein Hospice Inc. for supporting us in the creation of this book. We appreciate their dedication to provide comfort, compassion, and support during life's final journey. We consider ourselves honored and blessed to have been able to encounter so many inspiring patients and families. If not for our work with Stein Hospice—staff, patients, and families—this book would not have been possible. We are forever grateful.

We would also like to thank our family and friends for their love and support. It means more than words can say.

Table of Contents

Part I 13
   Preface 13
   Reflections of 15
   Family Tree 17
   My Roles through My Life 18
   Home and Community 20
   Friends 22
   Pets 24
   School Years 26
   Career 28
   Military Service 30
   Religion/Spirituality 32
   The Changing World 34
   Favorites 36
   Life's Gifts 37
   Special Memories 39
   Life Lessons 42
   Hopes and Fears 44
   After I Am Gone 45

Part II 49
   Anticipatory Grief 51
   Managing Caregiver Stress 53
   How to Comfort a Loved One Who Is Dying 57
   Normal Grief 63

Normal Grief Reactions 65

Theories of Grief and Loss 67

Grief Among the Ages 71

Information for Parents to Help a Grieving Child 73

Should Children Attend Funerals/Memorials? 75

Different Types of Loss 77

Helpful Suggestions for Coping with Grief and Loss 79

Complicated/Traumatic Grief 81

Coping with Grief on Special Days—Holidays, Anniversaries, Birthdays 85

References 89

Resources for Further Reading 91

Additional Resources for Children 93

For the Visitors 97

Memorial Service/Funeral 107

About the Authors 109

Endnotes 111

Preface

Everyone leaves a legacy. Not everyone realizes this. It is our hope that through you will come to an understanding of your own legacy. Every person should hav die knowing that their life had purpose and meaning. Unfortunately, we have see having that experience.

This book was created with the purpose of increasing your self-awareness ar coming together to talk about life and death. The book helps people complete a dying and their families together, and assists in having difficult conversations.

The first half of the book is designed for you to reflect on your life's story, wh by you or with others. Most sections will also include a picture page that will a own pictures related to the subject of each section. The second half of the book education and resources to help you during this time.

Although this work can be painful at times, it is important to facilitate healin is our hope that after completing this book, your knowledge gained from this lif as you transition into the next.

Name: _____

Place Picture Here

Date of Birth: _____

Born at _____ in _____
          (hospital)   (city)(state)

Today's Date: _____

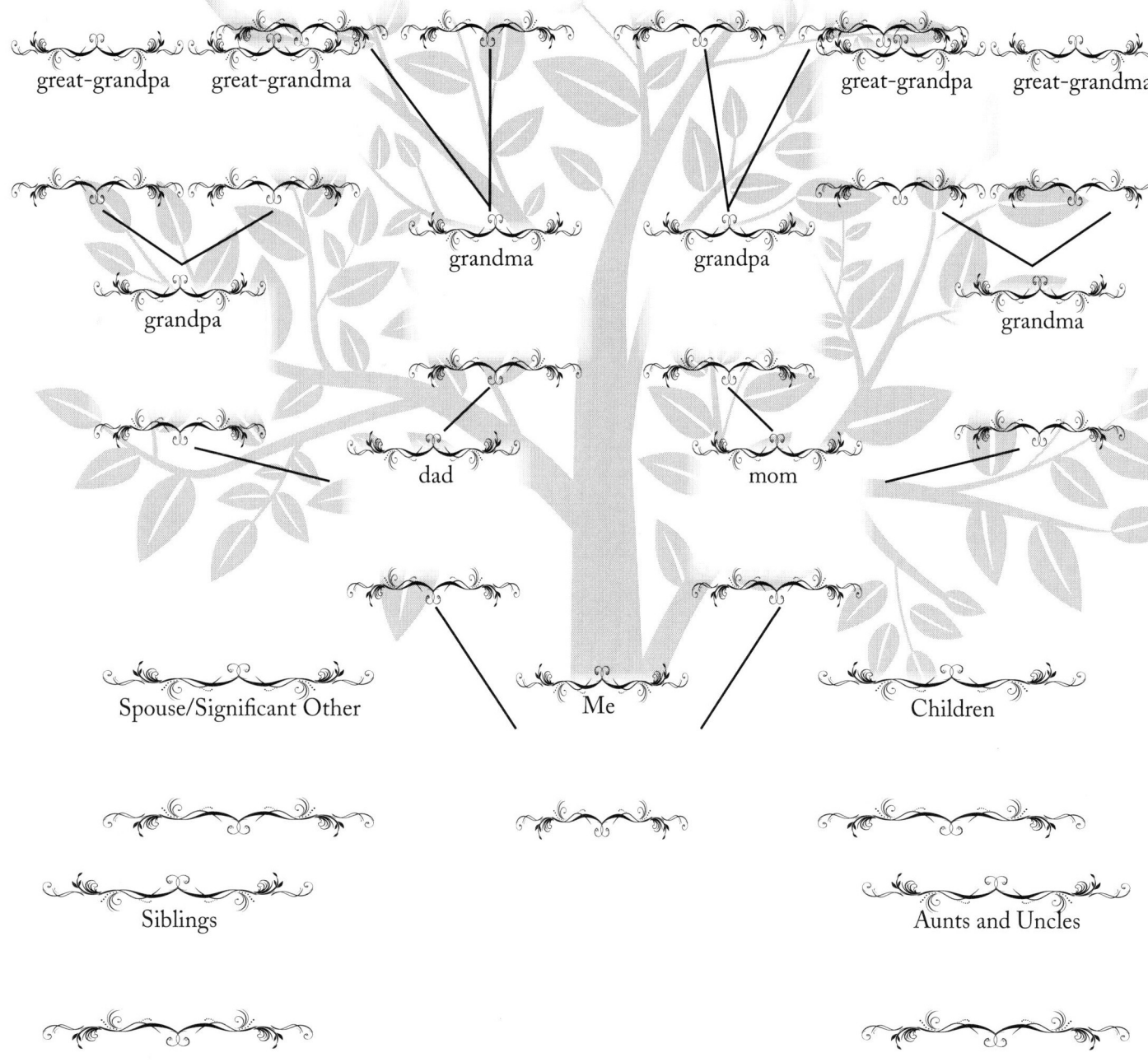

My Roles through My Life
Reflections of being a...

On the above lines, fill in each role you have experienced in your life and write a sentence or two reflecting on that role, for example, how did you feel in this role, what was your favorite part of this role, what do you remember about this role and when did you do this role:

- Child
- Sibling
- Spouse
- Parent
- Grandparent
- Great-Grandparent
- Friend
- Employee
- Volunteer
- Soldier/Family Member of Soldier
- Church Member
- Other

Home and Community

Location of my first home: _____

My age: _____

Who lived there: _____

My favorite and least favorite thing about this home: _____

_____

Description/thoughts of this community: _____

_____

Location of other homes:

My age: _____

Who lived there: _____

My favorite and least favorite thing about this home: _____

_____

Description/thoughts of this community: _____

_____

My home now:

My age: _____

Who lived there: _____

My favorite and least favorite thing about this home: _____

_____

Description/thoughts of this community: _____

_____

Roles Picture Page

Home and Community Picture Page

Friends

Friends of my lifetime and their characteristics: _____

_____

_____

_____

_____

_____

_____

_____

Special memories and things we did together: _____

_____

_____

_____

_____

_____

_____

What they taught me and how they changed me: _____

_____

_____

_____

_____

_____

_____

Friends Picture Page

Pets

Name: _____

Breed/type of pet/description: _____

Member of our family since: _____

Date of death: _____

Personality traits: _____

Memories/stories: _____

_____

Name: _____

Breed/type of pet/description: _____

Member of our family since: _____

Date of death: _____

Personality traits: _____

Memories/stories: _____

_____

Name: _____

Breed/type of pet/description: _____

Member of our family since: _____

Date of death: _____

Personality traits: _____

Memories/stories: _____

_____

Pets Picture Page

School Years

Suggestions: where you attended, how you got to school, how you liked or disliked school at this point, school friends, favorite and not-so-favorite teachers, grades, school activities—sports, band, clubs—and favorite memories.

Grade School: _____

_____

_____

_____

_____

Middle School: _____

_____

_____

_____

_____

High School: _____

_____

_____

_____

_____

College/Vocational: _____

_____

_____

_____

_____

School Years Picture Page

Career

What I wanted to be when I was a kid: _____

What I became as an adult: _____

First job (position, company, age): _____

Retired from (position, company, age): _____

Worst job and why: _____

_____

_____

Favorite job and why: _____

_____

_____

Favorite memories: _____

_____

_____

_____

_____

_____

Accomplishments/awards/achievements/proud moments/disappointments: _____

_____

_____

_____

_____

Career Picture Page

Military Service

Branch of service: _____

Years spent in the military: _____

Position(s): _____

Active duty/active combat: _____

Places traveled: _____

Honors/commendations: _____

Thoughts about service: _____

_____

_____

_____

_____

Reflections of my comrades: _____

_____

_____

_____

Best and worst parts, how it changed me: _____

_____

_____

_____

_____

Military Service Picture Page

Religion/Spirituality

Childhood faith traditions and upbringing: _____

Current faith traditions (i.e.—denomination, ritual practices, etc.): _____

Special memories surrounding my religion/spirituality: _____
_____
_____

Favorite hymn/prayer/scripture and its meaning to me: _____
_____
_____

Spiritual beliefs that I would like to pass on to future generations: _____
_____
_____
_____

Beliefs/thoughts of afterlife: _____
_____
_____
_____

Thoughts on forgiveness (am I open to receiving it, to giving it): _____
_____
_____

Religion/Spirituality Picture Page

The Changing World

How did prices compare from when you were younger until now?

- Gas: _____
- Groceries: _____
- Cars: _____
- Homes: _____
- College: _____
- Movies: _____
- Clothes: _____

World Events:

- Biggest shock as a nation: _____
- Our country's biggest changes: _____
- Our country's saddest moment: _____
- Our country's happiest moment: _____

- Important figures you admired and why: _____
  _____
  _____

- How any of these events affected my life or my family's life: _____
  _____
  _____
  _____

Politics:

- Favorite president and why: _____
- Least favorite president and why: _____
- Political affiliation: _____

- Thoughts on politics: _____
  _____
  _____
  _____

- Current president: _____
  _____
  _____
  _____

Favorites

TV show: _____

Movie: _____

Play: _____

Music: _____

Color: _____

Food: _____

Number: _____

Time of day: _____

Book (as child and as adult): _____

Animal: _____

Season: _____

Holiday: _____

Quote: _____

Recipe: _____

Fix-it tip: _____

Flower: _____

Car: _____

Hobbies: _____

Favorite sports: _____

Childhood memory: _____

Adult memory: _____

Celebration: _____

Place: _____

Surprise: _____

Life's Gifts

What do you consider to be the greatest gifts in your life (can be materialistic and non-materialistic gifts)? How did these gifts impact your life?

_____
_____
_____
_____
_____
_____
_____
_____
_____
_____
_____
_____
_____
_____
_____
_____
_____
_____
_____

Greatest gifts received:

_____
_____
_____
_____
_____
_____
_____
_____
_____
_____

Greatest gifts given:

_____
_____
_____
_____
_____
_____
_____
_____
_____
_____

Special Memories

Vacations: _____
_____
_____
_____

Holidays: _____
_____
_____
_____

Family traditions: _____
_____
_____
_____

Funniest moment(s): _____
_____
_____
_____

Most embarrassing moment(s): _____
_____
_____
_____

Happiest moment(s): _____

_____

_____

_____

Proudest moment(s): _____

_____

_____

_____

Special celebrations/events: _____

_____

_____

_____

Most life-changing moment(s): _____

_____

_____

_____

Other(s): _____

_____

_____

_____

Special Memories Picture Page

Life Lessons

What I used to value and think is important: _____

_____

_____

_____

_____

_____

_____

_____

Now what I value and know is important: _____

_____

_____

_____

_____

_____

_____

_____

Who has been influential in teaching me life lessons and why: _____

_____

_____

_____

_____

_____

_____

_____

_____

_____

The best advice about life to pass on to future generations: _____

_____

_____

_____

_____

_____

_____

_____

_____

_____

Hopes and Fears

My biggest fear: _____
_____
_____
_____
_____
_____
_____

My greatest hope: _____
_____
_____
_____
_____
_____
_____

What I can do about them: _____
_____
_____
_____
_____
_____
_____

After I Am Gone

Thoughts to my loved ones: _____

Things I would like you to remember about me: _____

Part 2:
Grief and Loss—Education and Resources

Anticipatory Grief

> There are things that we don't want to happen but have to accept, things we don't want to know but have to learn, and people we can't live without but have to let go.[1]
>
> —Author Unknown

Anticipatory grief refers to loss and grief reactions that can normally occur before an impending loss. It can be similar to the normal process of grieving, but it happens before the actual loss (in anticipation of death). Anticipatory grief can occur for the patient who has been given a terminal diagnosis and for their loved ones and friends, as they prepare for the many anticipated losses and changes to happen. Recognition of associated losses in the past, present, and future may begin.

Some of the losses felt in anticipatory grief for both the patient and their loved ones can be loss of social life, companionship, control, independence, and habits (i.e.—eating, sleeping, work, recreation, and routines). There may be fears related to life without the loved one and fear of the unknown. When a patient is grieving, they may begin to reflect on their life, to observe changes occurring, and to imagine how life will continue to change. Life review can be therapeutic for both the patient and their loved ones in the anticipatory grief process. Even though it can be painful, it can be helpful to talk about what the survivors are going to do after the death. Not only can some very practical planning be accomplished, the plan can provide reassurance to the person who is dying.

It is normal for people to experience a combination of recurring signs and symptoms of anticipatory grief, which may include tearfulness, anger, depression, anxiety, fear, guilt, constantly changing emotions, emotional numbness, poor concentration and focus, changes in sleeping and eating habits, forgetfulness, fatigue, denial, regret, peace, pride, and acceptance. Often people overlook anticipatory grief reactions and do not give time to experience the pain of their grief. It can be beneficial for healing to acknowledge your feelings and thoughts with those you feel comfortable talking to.

As a person is experiencing the emotions of anticipatory grief, they may feel empowered because they have an opportunity to say good-bye, express emotions, take care of unfinished business, forgive and seek forgiveness, express their wishes, do life review, which can help in providing reassurance that their life mattered, and show appreciation and love for each other. Anticipatory grief can prepare patients and their loved ones for the end of life, and death can happen in a more peaceful manner. However, it can be difficult if people begin to prematurely detach from their loved ones by withdrawing or isolating themselves from the dying person. Sometimes people will not share their emotions or process the end of life with their loved ones. Some reasons for this are that they want to *be strong* for others and do not want to *burden* anyone, or they may be attempting to avoid the pain of their grief. Unfortunately, anticipatory grief can be an emotional roller coaster for some, but recognizing and understanding this can help with coping.

It is important to note that not everyone experiences anticipatory grief. It does not mean a person loves any less if they do not experience this type of grief. Everyone copes with life and death differently. It is a very unique journey. Anticipatory grief does not mean that before a death a person feels the same kind of grief as the grief felt after a death. There is not a set amount of grief a person will feel. There is no right or wrong way of grieving, no script to follow or blueprint on how to grieve. The grieving process is unique to each person who experiences loss. Allowing oneself to grieve aids emotional and spiritual healing. When feelings are repressed, the feelings gain power; when feelings are embraced, you gain strength. Talk about your emotions and share your thoughts and feelings with those you feel comfortable with.

Managing Caregiver Stress

Courage is being afraid but going on anyhow.[2]

—Dan Rather

Caregivers often have a unique grief that is not only affected by personal emotions and reactions, but they continue to experience changes in their grief based on their loved one's condition. A caregiver continues to experience grief through their loved one's diagnosis and disease process. The disease can sometimes be lengthy, lasting several years. During this time, people may assume that the caregiver has enough time to adjust to the condition and accept the reality of decline. However, caregivers often continue to experience changes in their grief, based on the up and down conditions of their loved one's health.

Caregivers often overlook their own needs while providing care to their loved one. Caregivers do not think that there is time to address their own needs or feel selfish or guilty for taking their own time. Caregivers will often push themselves to their physical and emotional limitations without even recognizing it. It is important for caregivers to take care of themselves too. There are ways for family members to get support for themselves and keep in balance with caring for others. Here are some ideas:

Have realistic expectations about the disease It is important to obtain education about the terminal illness and condition. This helps a person to reach an understanding of their own limitations of what they will and will not be able to do in the care of their loved one. If your physician is hesitant to provide a prognosis, ask him or her to give you their best guess, with the understanding that this is a best guess.

Have realistic expectations about caregiving. Take pressure off yourself by managing stressors and changing daily activities. The house does not need to be kept the same, nor does the caregiver need to be a *host* for all of the company that comes through their house.

Have realistic expectations about relationship changes. Sometimes one of the greatest gifts to give a loved one is not to expect them to handle themselves in the same manner they have previously. They may be experiencing their own emotions and need to work through them in their own manner. Depending on the illness, they may find difficulty in remembering or accessing previous habits that brought comfort. A person may be grumpier or more detached than usual. This can be hard as caregivers to see these changes. Your loved one may have been regimented with watching their favorite sports team or going for a Sunday drive and now no longer shows an interest. Reassure your loved one that you do not have expectations of them during this time. Together you can work to meet both of your needs in a manner that meets your present circumstances, such as being together in silence or prayer.

Be open to joy. There continues to be moments of joy and love throughout the illness. It is important to not allow the stress and decline of your loved one's health to overshadow positive moments and to also allow yourself to experience the moments where love continues to be shared.

There are many items available that can assist with creating a safe environment. There can be items that will bring comfort to the caregiver and/or their loved one. A reacher is a tool that can be used to grab things that by overextending could cause pulled muscles or falls. Shower chairs can assist with taking pressure off of you and your loved one when cleaning. Removing rugs can prevent tripping and falling. Scan your environment to observe any fall or safety hazards, such as candles and sharp corners. There are also safety items available to assist with care and safety as the illness progresses. Grab bars can be used around the home to assist with mobility and staying support as your loved one moves through the home. There are corner cushions to pad sharp edges. Pillboxes can be used to keep track of days and times that medication is to be distributed. There are safety alarms available to alert you if your loved one has gotten up or fallen. Finding these resources can help you be prepared before situations arise.

Legal and financial planning. When legal and financial decisions are in place early in the illness it can relieve stress later when decisions would be forced to be made. Often a person feels overwhelmed in their stress as the illness continues, which can make it difficult to decide what they would like in regards to future planning. Therefore, you and your loved one can address matters such as wills and estate planning. Paperwork can be prepared to address your loved one's wishes for their own health code status. A power of attorney form can be completed for healthcare and/or financial matters so that there is a person(s) responsible for executing the patient's wishes and aware of what those wishes are in the event that the patient is unable to express their desires. While these are difficult subjects to discuss, it can allow for open communication about the disease process and thoughts and emotions being experienced through the illness. Once the patient's wishes are already known, it helps to alleviate stress at times when decisions need to be made.

Ask for and accept help. There are other people available and willing to help. By allowing others to share in the care, it will help to give a much needed break to get other personal errands done or to rest. This is also an opportunity to help those around to get fulfillment by assisting you. Be specific with what you need. You may need help with the physical care of your loved one, with running errands, sitting with your loved one and giving you a break, cleaning, cooking, caring for children in the home, organizing and planning, etc.

Have humor in the day. Laughter can help bring positive perspective in a person's life. Seeing the lighter side of things helps a person to cope.

Connect with others. Not only is it important to have support from others with caregiving so you can get a break, but it is also important to be with others. A person needs emotional and social connections. It is important to be with someone who is trusted and who would be supportive. This connection can be a time to share emotions about the situation, enjoy a recreational activity, or participate in a support group.

Learn to control what causes stress. Establish limits! Identify what is possible to change and what cannot be changed. Focus on using slow, deep, and mindful breathing throughout the day. Slowing down breathing patterns helps to slow down your heart rate and pulse rate; it also lowers blood pressures and relaxes muscles.

Recognize physical signs of stress. Stress can be manifested in a physical manner. Physical manifestations can be muscle tightness or back aches. There may be ongoing headaches. A person's weight and sleeping may increase or decrease. It is important to eat and rest well and continue to have routine physician appointments.

Identify warning signs of stress. A person may experience a range of stressful emotions, such as denial, anxiety, depression, irritability, or anger. Caregivers may begin to withdraw from people or activities they had enjoyed. A person may feel chronically exhausted and experience health problems.

Accept and share feelings. There are many emotions that can be experienced with grief and all of them are normal. It is important to acknowledge these feelings and confide honestly in a trusted person. Another way of releasing emotions can be through writing in a personal journal.

Time management. There are often many tasks to complete, and it can feel overwhelming. It can be useful to make a priority list and rank them. Begin with completing the essentials and identifying any tasks that can be eliminated or assigned to someone else.

Spiritual renewal. Find time to pray or meditate. This can be done through private meditation, prayer, joining a faith community, or getting out in nature.

Access personal supports. Make a list of personal stress relievers. Put the list in a place that will be accessible and serve as a reminder of coping skills. Relieve yourself of unreasonable expectations that you may have; for example—that you can be all things to all people all the time. Instead, accept your humanity and your need to depend on others now. Let someone take you away now and then for some *stress relief.*

Indulge. Get a massage, eat out, or find any activity to treat yourself because you are worth it.

Take time for yourself. It is important as a caregiver to be in touch with personal needs. Look for activities that bring inner peace and are calming, such as reading, listening to music, or going for a walk. Take time to begin to apply some of these coping strategies to your life.

How to Comfort a Loved One Who Is Dying

Those whom we loved never really leave us. They live on forever in our hearts and cast their radiant light onto every shadow.[3]

—Sylvana Rossetti

It is normal to want to ensure our loved ones are comfortable and at peace as death approaches. There are several normal occurrences in the dying process that begin before the final day or hour of your loved one's life. Knowledge about the normalcy of these symptoms can help to prepare you and your loved ones to get everything you need from the dying process. The following information gives some ideas on how to provide support to your loved ones and yourself during these times.

Withdrawal. At the end of life it is natural to see a dying person start to withdraw from their usual routines, family, and friends. You may notice they start to sleep more and not talk as much. Sometimes they can appear to be unresponsive and can be difficult to arouse. This is a natural part of the dying process as the dying are preparing to depart from this physical world and are beginning to let go. Sleeping can provide an opportunity to continue to do life's work in dreams and resolve any unresolved issues. Dreams allow for people to go outside of time and space. This task requires a lot of energy. It is important work because it prepares them for the next phase of life.

As a loved one, it is difficult to experience this stage because you want to be with them and continue to share everything. There are ways you can provide support to them without disrupting their sleep and need to withdraw. You can allow for them to take their time to rest. You can give them the sense of your presence through touch rather than conversation. Prepare for visits at times that the patient seems to be more alert. Encourage everyone to identify the names of visitors in a clear and normal tone when visiting with the dying person. Limit the environmental stimulants such as the television, loud noises, and visitors when you see your loved one getting tired. Remember that your loved one can still hear even if they do not seem responsive.

Agitation. This stage can be difficult for loved ones to experience because they hope death will be peaceful. When a person is agitated, the person may be restless because they continue to be in motion.

You may notice them become restless, such as picking at sheets, their clothes, and doing the same motion over and over. Restlessness occurs because circulation is slowing and they are receiving less oxygen to the brain. Agitation can also be indicative of emotional, spiritual, or physical pain.

There are many ways to support someone experiencing agitation. You can provide presence through soft touch, such as holding hands or putting your hand on their heart. You can provide comfort by speaking calmly and in a soothing manner. You can soften any environmental stimulants and soothe them with inspirational and soft music, as well as limiting the loud noises like television. Remember that your loved one may no longer find comfort in familiar shows or songs as they let go of some aspects of this physical world. They will not be upset if the television is off even if it has been on for the last forty years. You can read or share fond memories with them. For safety purposes, it can be useful to install bed railings. It may also be necessary to have someone always sitting with them, or to use a baby monitor. Make sure that you do not overexert yourself by working to physically comfort the patient or restrain them. Take shifts with someone else to sit with your loved one so that you can get the rest you need. Like all symptoms, it is important to report agitation to medical staff when these symptoms arise. There are also social, emotional, and spiritual supports that may be utilized to provide comfort to the patient.

Confusion. This stage of the dying process used to be mistaken as a result of the medications being administered, but confusion and disorientation is a common stage of the dying process. Frequently, people begin to report seeing things or people (already deceased or who have not been there to visit) that are not observed by others in the physical world. People may begin to carry on conversations with their loved ones that have died. They may be doing some life review or spiritual work and can go back and forth between the past and present, between this world and the next, if you will. This time can be a painful and beautiful experience for all involved because it creates an opportunity to have a look into the next life as well as get insight about life after death. Confusion may be allowing them to express emotions that may have been repressed. It can also be the result of a lack of oxygen to the brain. During this time you can work to affirm what the person is experiencing as this is a real experience for them. It will be useful to state your name, place, and timeframe to continue to orient the person to where they are. You can offer comfort to them by reassuring them that they are loved and have people to take care of them and that they are not alone. If needed and appropriate, you can limit visitors.

Appetite changes. When a person begins to lose interest in food and drink, this can be an extremely difficult stage for loved ones to accept and support. Your loved one may not experience any appetite, or only have some cravings. This can be a struggle for caregivers because they associate food as a way to help the dying person gain strength. In reality, it can cause more pain than help. Society has expectations that food helps a person to become stronger and healthier, but this is not the case in the dying process. The body is beginning to slow down and is not able to process foods the way it used to. There can be weight loss that occurs normally during the dying process, and it does not mean the body is not getting what it needs. A person will indicate when they are experiencing hunger or thirst, and they will not starve themselves to death.

As a loved one, this is a stage where it can be a struggle to determine the difference between supporting and encouraging eating and drinking, as opposed to forcing them to eat. Be gentle with yourself and allow the person to dictate what they want and when they want it. They know their body and will take food and fluid as needed. It is no longer about nutritional value of food, but their enjoyment of the food. The dying tend to prefer liquids over solid foods because it's easier to take in. If the person is able to swallow, you can provide small amounts of liquid through a straw method. Place your thumb over one end of the straw and transfer the liquid. Small chips of ice, frozen liquids, or popsicles can be enjoyable. The taste or smell of food may provide comfort even if the person is unable to swallow or eat. So you can continue to eat while sitting with your loved one. They will let you know if they want to eat. They will also display signs when they are not hungry. Signs may include biting down on the spoon, spitting out food, or turning their heads. Respect the person's choice to refuse food and relieve them of the expectation that they have to eat.

Changes in elimination. There are many circumstances that affect changes in elimination. These include eating less, having fewer physical movements, taking pain medications, and changes in circulation. As the body is shutting down, the muscles begin to relax and a person begins to lose control of their bladder and bowels. The urine output may decrease because they take in fewer liquids. When they urinate, the urine could be darker, cloudy, or have a strong odor. Sometimes people experience a high output of urine even after they have ceased fluid intake due to fluid shifts in the body.

During this time, loved ones work to maintain the patient's dignity by keeping the patient dry and comfortable. Disposable briefs and under pads may be necessary. Be sure to check your loved one frequently to ensure they are dry. Lotions and creams can be applied to the skin periodically to provide additional comfort. Use of stool softeners or laxatives may assist in *regular* bowel functions, but this is not the case in the dying process. Bowel eliminations may decrease as the body is shutting down. Continue to speak to medical staff about the changes noticed and if laxatives are needed or appropriate.

Changes in circulation. As the circulation system begins to shut down, it becomes more centralized. The outermost circulation will diminish (hands and feet) and limbs begin to feel cool. There may be swelling or discoloration in the limbs. Another complication with circulation changes is bedsores. A bedsore will occur when a person is located in the same position for hours at a time.

This is another important stage to continue to be in contact with the medical staff to let them know changes noticed in the body coloring and temperature. This is a time to continue to focus on rotating the position of your loved one to avoid developing bedsores. This should be done every two to four hours. It does not need to be a whole new position, but a change of the pressure points. There are special mattresses and pads that can be used as well. Also, work to keep the skin clean and dry. Provide gentle massaging with good lotion. However, even with the best care, bedsores are sometimes unavoidable.

Body temperature changes. In addition to circulation changes, there can also be body temperature changes. Sometimes the body can be hotter and sometimes cooler. With this there can be skin color changes. Sometimes a gray or purple look can develop, and skin can look spotted or blotchy.

There are ways to continue to meet the needs of your loved one when their body temperature changes. If they have a fever you can use a cool washcloth on the forehead, under the armpits, around the neck, or in the groin. Evaluate if they have excess blankets as you may remove some. Respect if your loved one is removing covers as this may indicate they feel warm, even with no signs of a fever, and opening a window or using a fan may help. For a cool body temperature, a warmed blanket can help, but do not use an electric blanket.

Changes in breathing. You may notice that your loved one's breathing patterns change as they near the end of their life. Breathing may slow down or can rapidly increase and be shallow, followed by periods of no breaths. The changes in a person's breath does not cause someone discomfort. A *rattling* sound can occur as a person draws toward the end of their life. A person can become so weak that they lose their ability to swallow or cough and will have saliva and mucus gather in the back of the throat, causing this rattling sound. This sound is usually more disturbing to caregivers and does not cause discomfort to the person. People inquire about suctioning, but this will usually increase the secretions and cause discomfort. Often, hours prior to death, the breathing patterns turn to regular, deep, and panting breaths. A final breath will be a gasping of the mouth where there is little to no intake of air, followed by sighs.

There are ways to assist your loved one as they experience these changes. Gently turn them on their side to assist with draining secretions. It can also be helpful to elevate the head of the bed. There are medications that may assist in drying excess secretions. Medications can be prescribed by a physician if the breathing seems to be labored or painful. You can also provide good mouth care—because a person's mouth becomes dry when breathing with their mouth open—by using mouth swabs.

Surge of energy. It is not unusual, at some point during the dying process, for the dying person to have a burst of energy where they seem alert and maybe even better. They may request to eat or be very talkative. This could also come in the form of a small conversation or a few words spoken from someone who has not been responsive for some time. This can be confusing to family and friends because they may think the dying person is taking a turn for the better. However, it is quite commonly seen soon before death and may be a last good-bye. Since you have been under a lot of stress, this stage may be confusing and bring hope that your loved one is recovering. Enjoy this time instead of questioning whether different care needs to be provided. Your loved one will indicate what they need through words or actions. Allow this to be a time to say good-byes and reminisce as needed. Be affectionate. Hold hands and hug as appropriate. Let there be silent moments of togetherness.

Saying good-bye. This is a difficult task for any loved one, and often a person will deliberate when and how to accomplish this. People struggle with when is an appropriate time because they do not want to feel they are encouraging their loved one to die, or upsetting them by giving them permission to die. It can be a challenge to find the words. Also, people work to give permission to their loved ones that it is okay to let go. You may want to tell your loved one how proud you are of their journey and the strength they have shown during this time. Tell them it is okay to go to their eternal home when they are ready. You can reassure them that you will always carry their love with you. This can be an intense and emotional time for all involved.

As difficult as it is, make sure that you are saying what you need to say during this process. Speak from your heart. You can tell them how much you cherish them and your memories. You can also be honest that it is hard to let go of holding their hand, but know that they hold your heart always. There are no magic words to take away the pain of this process for you or your loved one. Focus on the love you share in these moments. This may be an opportunity to say apologies or forgive and let go of past conflicts. It can also be time to express gratitude and appreciations. Remember that the dying person can hear even when they do not appear to be responsive. It is okay for tears to come. Tears are a normal part of the dying process. Allow them to come because it can be a healthy expression of the love you share and pain you feel, releasing internal stress. Understand that not everyone cries and this is not an indication that there is no love or pain.

With all of these stages, and through the dying process, it is important to allow yourself and your loved ones the opportunity to maximize the time you have together. There are not any "supposed to's." This is a guide to assist you through this difficult time in your life; however, keep in mind that everyone responds differently to loss, grief, and change.

Normal Grief

Grief is itself a medicine.[4]

—William Cowper

Before and after the death of a loved one it is natural to feel intense and painful emotions associated with the loss. The emotions that are experienced during the grieving process are important in helping a person recognize the loss and adjust to the many changes experienced. Grief is universal, but there is uniqueness with each individual's grief. Grief can be affected by the nature of the relationship between the deceased and the bereaved. Normal grief is not an illness or pathological condition. It is a natural reaction to the loss of something or someone that we prized, loved, and cared for. We grieve because we love.

The circumstances that surround the death can influence a person's grief. A person grieves based on their unique personality, as well as the influence of the deceased's unique personality. The bereaved spiritual beliefs, culture, and gender all can influence the grief experienced. The funeral and/or memorial service can affect a person's grief. With so many factors influencing a person's grief, no two people will grieve in the exact same manner. Bereaved individuals face the challenge of working to experience the pain of their loss while continuing to take care of themselves. Grieving is stressful and takes enormous energy. A person experiencing this grief may notice that grief can affect them on a physical, cognitive, emotional, social, and spiritual level.

Normal grief is like waves in the lake or ocean, the waves of grief tide in and out. Sometimes you get hit by a small wave, sometimes you get hit by a large wave, and sometimes you are in the middle of the store and are hit by a wave that you did not see coming and you break down crying. We never get over our grief; it is a lifelong process. We do eventually learn how to live with our loss, adapt to it, and find hope, meaning, and purpose to our life again. It depends on what you do with your grief; it is not the passage of time that heals but what you do with the time. Grieving requires you to be an active participant. The only way out is through our pain, through our grief. In ways, you are trying to hold light and dark at the same time. You are going from an old normal to a new normal and when you are grieving you are trying to figure out what is your new normal. There can be healing and growth as a result of our grief; in this way, grief is the cure.

Normal Grief Reactions

There is a sacredness in tears. They are not the mark of weakness, but of power. They speak more eloquently than ten thousand tongues. They are messengers of overwhelming grief…and unspeakable love.[5]

—Washington Irving

Physical: A person can experience the stress of their grief by having physical manifestations, such as headaches, upset stomach, muscle aches, pains, an increased/decreased appetite, changing sleep patterns, tightness and tension throughout the body, oversensitivity to noise, shortness of breath, feelings of being outside of oneself or shakiness, changes in blood pressure and heart rate, urinary frequency, and bowel movements or menstrual cycle changes. The stress of grief may cause current medical conditions to become intensified. It is important to get routine medical care and check with your doctor regarding any physical reactions.

Cognitive: When a person is experiencing the stress of grief, they may feel like their mind is beginning to go *crazy*, as many grievers have stated. A bereaved individual may become preoccupied with a person or thing. The person may begin to have a sense of the presence of the deceased. They may have difficulty concentrating or focusing, experience memory lapses, or become more aware of their own mortality.

Emotional: There are several emotions that can be experienced with grief. The emotions associated with grief can feel like a roller coaster and there is no predictable order or time frame for them. A person may experience sadness, loneliness, guilt, self-doubt, and self-blame. A person can experience relief, shock, and numbness. Other emotions may be anger, resentment, bitterness, hurt, and anxiety. With grief, a person can feel helpless, blame others, feel empty, or feel confused.

Social: When a person is grieving, they may have difficult times adjusting to the changes in their social setting. A person may feel isolated and not want to hang out with the usual friends and acquaintances. People can find support from acquaintances and may be surprised with whom they find support.

Spiritual: A person's faith can become intensified with their grief. A person may find peace in their thoughts about the afterlife. Another common reaction with grief is that a person may question their beliefs about the afterlife and a person's suffering and death. It is important to continue to explore spiritual beliefs and get support as needed.

Theories of Grief and Loss

My grief and pain are mine. I have earned them. They are part of me. Only in feeling them do I open myself to the lessons that they can teach.[6]

—Anne Wilson Schaef

Elizabeth Kübler-Ross (1969) describes five stages of grief. These stages have been identified as being common to many people who are coping with a terminal prognosis, although they can be experienced in bereavement as well. Individuals will not necessarily experience all the stages and can experience them simultaneously. The grief process does not necessarily follow a linear pattern. Grieving is a cyclical process that moves back and forth on an emotional continuum.

Denial: In this stage the individual is not yet ready to experience the reality of the prognosis. Denial is a natural defense mechanism the mind uses to avoid becoming overwhelmed with the intensity of the situation. Many people in this stage may say, "This isn't happening to me!" Others may minimize the severity of the illness or its prognosis.

Anger: Anger can serve a purpose in a person's grief and may manifest in various manners. A person's anger may be directed at themselves for not being able to overcome this disease or guilt that they did something to bring this upon themselves. A person may feel angry at their loved ones, at medical professionals, and/or God. Many people in this stage may ask, "Why is this happening to me?" Anger can also cover up emotional pain.

Bargaining: This stage is where a person works to bargain with God or a higher power to allow them more time on earth. Many people in this stage may say, "I promise I will be a better person if…" People may feel like there are things they can do to earn a different diagnosis.

Depression: At this point in a person's grief, they have begun to accept the reality of the situation and are experiencing the pain and intensity of normal grief emotions (sadness, loneliness, guilt, regret, worry, and reflection). Many people in this stage may say, "I don't care anymore."

Acceptance: This is when a person has accepted the reality, worked through the emotions, and a more peaceful feeling begins. Many people in this stage may say, "I am ready for whatever comes."

J. William Worden, PhD (2009), describes four tasks of grieving, more specifically related to grief following a loss. His theory projects that a person must mourn the death of someone who has been significant in his or her life. That if mourning is not complete, growth and development cannot take place and lifetime complications could develop. As with Elizabeth Kubler Ross's stages, these tasks do not necessarily occur in an exact order. Those who are grieving may go back and forth between two or three tasks while doing grief work. There is no set amount of time that these tasks take, but it is usually seen over months and years, versus days or weeks.

To accept the reality of the loss. Even when death is expected there is still a feeling that it did not happen. This task involves recognizing that the person is dead and will not return. Death must be accepted on an intellectual and emotional level. Rituals, such as funerals and talking about the loss, can help the bereaved to begin to accept this.

To work through the pain of grief. We must feel the pain of our grief. The intensity of the pain and the way it is experienced and expressed is different for everyone. However, it is virtually impossible not to feel some amount of pain when someone very close to us dies. Friends and family are sometimes uncomfortable with this expression of pain and may try to interrupt this task. Grievers themselves may try to avoid this task by masking the pain through the use of alcohol or drugs, idealizing the deceased, avoiding reminders of the deceased, or by relocating or quickly getting into a new relationship. No matter how successful a griever is in avoiding the pain, it will eventually come back again.

To adjust to a new environment where the deceased person is missing. This is the stage where grievers struggle with all the changes that happen as a result of the person being gone. This includes the practical parts of daily living and are sometimes termed secondary losses, such as more responsibilities at home, living alone, raising children alone, facing an empty house, managing home maintenance and finances, and caring for oneself completely. During this task, the griever is feeling the effects their loss has upon their sense of who they are and how they see the world. The griever may suddenly feel that life is not fair and that people do not understand them anymore. During this task, there can be a sense of helplessness, inadequacy, and incapacity as one tries to adjust to living with the loss. The griever is trying to make sense of the loss and trying to regain some control over his or her life in this stage.

To emotionally relocate the deceased and move on with life. During this stage, grievers are acknowledging the value of the relationship they had with the deceased, everything they may have learned, loved, respected, or disagreed with about them. It is recognized that the deceased is not forgotten, nor the memories, and that it is okay to care and connect to others and continue to live their life. They can reinvest the energy in life, relax the ties to the deceased, and develop a new type of relationship with the deceased—one based on memory and spirit. In this stage, the griever does not have to give up their relationship with the deceased but finds an appropriate place for the deceased in their emotional life—a place that enables them to go on living effectively in the world. Sometimes this task can be hindered by holding onto the past attachment rather than going on and forging new ones. Some grievers find loss so painful that they make a pact with themselves to never love again. However, with time, and actively participating in grieving, the pain can lessen and the griever can redefine himself or herself.

Therese Rando, Ph.D., (1993) developed a grief model known as the Six R's:

Recognize the loss, which she describes as the need for people to first experience their loss and understand it happened.

React. People react emotionally to their loss; they react to the separation.

Recollect and re-experience. People may review memories of their lost relationship, events that occurred, shared experiences, or moments together. They recollect and re-experience the deceased and the relationship.

Readjust. The loss starts to feel less acute and people begin the process of returning to daily life. They readjust to and move adaptively into the new world, without forgetting the old.

Reinvest. People re-enter the world, ultimately forming new relationships and committing to their new life. They accept the changes that have occurred and move forward.

Grief Among the Ages

To live in the hearts we leave behind is not to die.[7]

—Thomas Campbell

Birth to three-year-olds: Babies and toddlers can sense when others are upset, as well as notice when there is a significant change in their life, such as the death of an involved person in their lives. They may show their grief through a lack of appetite, sleeping pattern changes, anger outbursts, crying, and becoming withdrawn. It is important to provide consistency with caretakers and maintain normal routines as much as possible.

Four- to six-year-olds: This age group has a limited understanding of death. They will not understand the finality of death and may confuse death with sleeping. A child this age will wonder about how a person continues to function (eating, using the bathroom, etc.) after they die. Explain death in physical terms, such as the heart stops beating and the body no longer moves. A child may inquire about going to heaven if the body is in the ground. This is a time to explain that the love/spirit of this person lives on. Children may have a regression in their behaviors, such as: bedwetting, thumb sucking, and temper tantrums. They begin to demonstrate anxiety. Caregivers can assist children in dealing with their emotions by allowing the children to express their emotions. Express them through role playing with dolls, stuffed animals, toy cars, or drawing pictures of their emotions. Caregivers can identify and help children learn the name of the emotions during this time so they can continue to identify them. While grieving, children need simple routines with a lot of affection and patience (especially as they regress in their behaviors). It is important to continue to allow time for the child to play.

Seven- to eleven-year-olds: When children are this age, they are able to articulate their emotions even if they may not be able to relate them to the grief. Children may act out in school by getting into more fights or struggling to remain focused on tasks. They may also regress in their behaviors (bedwetting, troubled appetites, nightmares, and waking up through the night). They may become afraid of death, as they understand the finality of death. They can become fearful that death could take another person that they love, but they are still not thinking it could actually happen to them. A child may also experience exaggerated physical symptoms or believe they have an imaginary illness. It is important to encourage children to express their emotions. They need reinforcement that they are not to blame for this death and that death is not a punishment for their behavior. It is also important to reinforce that the deceased person did not choose to leave them. Children are curious about death and will ask questions. As a child continues to grow in this age range, they begin to develop a deeper understanding of the concept of life and death and apply it to plants and animals. Continue to provide them with love and support and allow for them to help support and comfort others too. Children continue to need a routine during this time with the ongoing support of releasing their emotions through words and healthy actions.

Twelve- to eighteen-year-olds: This age group does not want to think about death and does not believe that it will happen to them or their loved ones. Teenagers may partake in risky behaviors because they believe they and others are invincible. When a death occurs and a teenager is grieving, they may take more risks or demonstrate acting out behaviors. Like other age groups, they may experience trouble sleeping or oversleeping, eating too much or not enough, and struggle to concentrate. They not only experience their own loss, but are able to have empathy for the pain that their loved ones are experiencing. Teenagers will often turn to their peers for support. They struggle to feel understood in general, so they need to have their own support person that can be empathetic to their experience. Often this support person will not be a family member because teenagers often feel more comfortable relating to someone outside of their family. They may struggle with common emotions of grief, such as guilt, anger, sadness, loneliness, and questioning spiritual beliefs. Teenagers need to be given honest information, education, and modeling of how to cope in a positive manner.

Adults: Adults often begin to review their own lives when faced with the death of others. Some adults will evaluate their goals, relationships, and their own situations to explore if they are prioritizing their life as they would want. Other adults are unable to face the intensity of the situation and will work to avoid the emotions (overworking, shopping, substance use). Adults need to grieve, but they often feel compelled to be *strong* for others and work to support everyone else instead of addressing their own needs. Adults may become more irritable and sensitive.

Elderly: This age group is no longer focused on upcoming milestones they want to achieve; they reflect on the past. Grief for the elderly can be intense as they have continued to experience more losses the older they become. They may have a multitude of losses quickly and become overwhelmed. The elderly are not only dealing with the loss of relationships through death, but also multiple losses, such as their own health changes, end of careers, residence changes, and family changes. With all of these stressors, an elderly person may feel overwhelmed with their grief and unable to function or express their emotions.

Information for Parents to Help a Grieving Child

Weeping is perhaps the most human and universal of all relief measures.[8]

—Dr. Karl Menninger

Be honest. Be honest with a child. Use language that is age appropriate and accurately describes the permanency and reality of the death. For example, do not use the phrase the deceased is *sleeping* as this confuses a child by thinking that the deceased could wake up or that they could die if they go to sleep.

Listen to the child. Allow the child to share their thoughts or questions. This helps the child to begin the grieving process. Address what they want to know more information about. Allow them to share their stories and emotions without passing judgment or instructing them on how they should feel.

Allow the child to see your own grief. When children witness others' reactions to grief, such as sadness and crying, it normalizes their own instincts and gives them permission to release their own feelings.

Share memories. It is healing to share stories and memories. Sharing stories can be done on an ongoing basis, as well as on holidays and anniversaries.

Allow children to participate in rituals. Children can benefit from participating in rituals to help bring closure and accept the reality of the situation. They can also participate through writing a letter or drawing pictures (which can be placed in the casket). Commonly, when children are left out they imagine the worst.

Provide support. Most importantly with children, they need reassurance that even though things will be different, they will continue to be loved, cared for, and that you will work with them to figure out how to get through the loss.

Take respites from grief. Children need breaks from their emotions. Allow them to enjoy activities, as well as express their grief.

Should Children Attend Funerals/Memorials?

What we have once enjoyed and deeply loved we can never lose, for all that we love deeply becomes a part of us.[9]

—Helen Keller

There are many factors to consider when evaluating if a child should attend a funeral, and there is not one correct answer. Each family has their own culture as well as the need to look at the individuality of each child. However, these are some general guidelines to consider:

Evaluate the child's temperament and understanding. A child's understanding of death may help to decide if it is appropriate for them to attend. Children need to grieve as well, but if children are too young they may be distressed by seeing others upset, without understanding the loss.

Give the child the option. If a child is of an appropriate age and maturity level, they can be given the option if they would like to attend the service. Children should be provided with honest and age-appropriate education about the service and emotions that may be seen at the funeral. They should also be provided with clear information about the finality of death as they may become confused when seeing the deceased's physical body. Take time to discuss this information with the child. Make a decision based on their feedback as well as your own awareness of their grief and coping. Also, a child can be given the option if they would like to have any items from the deceased. If a child declines taking any personal items and you believe they may like something in the future, this could be set aside for a later date. Giving children options can empower them in their own grief.

Recognize potential learning tools from attending the memorial service/funeral. Children can benefit from witnessing grief and coping mechanisms people utilize. When children are aware of the intensity of others' emotions, it helps them to recognize death is serious and begin to understand emotions that are associated with grief. Children also learn there are different ways to handle grief through the emotions they witness at the funeral/memorial service. Be sure to use simple terms and give clear and honest information about the funeral.

Children work to attempt to understand and apply mortality. As children go through the grieving process, children learn to recognize the finality of death and that death will affect all people at some point. Funerals provide an opportunity for children to say good-bye and work through their own grief.

Evaluate if there are some events that children should engage in. It may be beneficial to have the child participate in only certain aspects of the ceremony based on other grievers' coping styles or the nature and intensity of ritual service. When children are able to engage in services, it allows for them to feel a part of the service, to grieve, and to give support. When a child is present, there should be a person available to address their needs and allow them to ask questions as they arise. You may want to task someone with the job of touching base regularly with the child at the service. If a child does not attend, they can show support through assisting in cooking or sending/making a card for the family.

Identify needs of the deceased. If the family would be uncomfortable with a child at the memorial, then it is important to respect this. As a caregiver, you can look into other options for creating a ritual for the child. The child may be able to go with you privately to the funeral home to say good-bye. You could complete a memorial project with the child to be taken to the funeral or displayed in the child's room, such as a picture collage. The child could also write a letter to the deceased.

Consider the length of the event. It is important to consider how long an event will occur because young children have a difficult time remaining quiet for extended periods of time.

Consider if there will be an open coffin or cremation. If the body will be viewed, it is important to inform the child as well as provide honest information about the physical body, such as the cold temperature, he/she will not move or talk, he/she may have new markings or smells, and the body may feel hard if they touch it. If there will be a cremation, explain what this means. Be sure to reiterate that the person is deceased and does not experience any pain in either of these processes.

Different Types of Loss

I thought that your death was a waste and a destruction, a pain of grief hardly to be endured. I am beginning to learn that your life was a gift and a growing and a loving left with me.[10]

—Marjorie Holburn

Death of a child: A child embodies their own unique personality, along with the hopes for their future. When a child dies before their parent, the parent feels the loss and emptiness of this missing hope. A parent grieves the death of their child regardless of the child's age, whether the death occurs through a miscarriage, stillbirth, or if the child is a young child or adult. When a parent outlives their child, it is out of the normal, anticipated, lifecycle events. The death of a child is an intense grief that can leave grievers at high risk for loss of family support, isolation, and feelings of hopelessness. A grieving parent strives to find a way to live their life with purpose, but they can also feel compelled to remain in the pain of the grief as a way to stay connected with the loss of their child. The pain of this grief can be so overwhelming because a parent identifies that a part of themselves died with their child. Along with their own identity changing, the whole family dynamic changes with the death of a child, as siblings adapt to a missing member. The whole family must work together to deal with their own emotions as well as adjust to their new roles in the family. Each family member has different relationships with this child, which impacts how they grieve. For example, a miscarriage means the baby was in the womb and the mother had an opportunity to have more time with the baby in a manner that is different than the father and other siblings. The family dynamics are also impacted by how open the parents are to grieve their child and changes in their family. A parent can be so consumed in their own pain that they cannot address the losses or changes going on around them. Another example would be a parent that works to remain so strong for their family that they work to maintain everything to be *normal* and do not share about the loss and changes being experienced. It is hard to accept comfort and support from others, especially as typical grief phrases are not found reassuring. Bereaved parents will often work to find some purpose in their child's death by providing acknowledgments of their child through ongoing gifts and memorials. While there can be various emotions in all grief, it is universal that an intense sadness and pain is experienced with the death of a child.

Death of a spouse: When a person chooses to become married, they have made a decision to join lives with someone. Often, there is much preparation for the union of two people, and not much focus on how this will affect the separation of their physical beings through death. A person often identifies losing a part of themselves when they lose their spouse. In a relationship, there are often roles that each partner assumes. With grief, a person can struggle as they work to transition to life without the physical presence of their partner, as well as learning new roles. In grief there are secondary losses experienced outside of losing the physical presence of the deceased. There are numerous secondary losses that can be experienced, such as learning to balance the checkbook, do yard work, cook, or handle car repairs. The stress of grief, in addition to learning new roles, can be overwhelming. Another loss suffered is that the deceased spouse is usually someone the bereaved could speak to or find comfort with in times of stress, and now their spouse is gone. It can be difficult to spend time with friends as it may have been a couple's group. A bereaved individual works to develop a new identity, yet constantly receives reminders about their loved one (mail, joint bank accounts, etc.). Also, when a spouse dies the bereaved spouse can experience pressures from family members to make changes, such as moving to a smaller home or a new town closer to other family members. In general, it is recommended that no major decisions be made immediately after death like moving, remarrying, etc.

Death of a parent: No matter what age a person is, when a child is with their parents, they will often revert to the roles of parent and child. When an adult child loses a parent, their grief may be disregarded because it is expected that parents will die, so not as much support is given or seen as needed. When a person loses their parent, they can still be overwhelmed with their emotions. Regardless of a person's age, they want their parents present at important milestones in their life. A parent is often someone who gave the bereaved unconditional love and support, and the bereaved now feels that loss. The parent may not have been an involved or supportive parent, and the bereaved child now finds that they are left facing those issues and feelings. There may be a lot of reflection about what was and was not said to them. A child may evaluate their own actions and experience guilt for the way they behaved. A bereaved child also deals with the family's structural change. The child may go from being the middle generation to being the eldest generation for the family.

Death of a sibling: Often, this loss is overlooked by society. Siblings are often seen as secondary mourners and the focus is given to the parents, children, and/or spouse of the deceased. Siblings are a part of each other's lives from birth on. They share a common history and genetics. Siblings help each other to develop identities, and when a sibling dies, a person may question their own roles and identity. Siblings may go from having another sibling to share thoughts with and share support, to being an only child. It is important for siblings to be able to express their grief in a supportive environment.

Helpful Suggestions for Coping with Grief and Loss

If life is a journey, then dealing with the death of a loved one, is one of those steep, rocky mountain roads that you don't know if you have the strength to climb up and over. The only way is one step at a time, moment by moment, and eventually you are on top of the mountain with an easier path to follow.[11]

—Patricia Rose Upczak

Understanding the grieving process: Often a person may feel like they are going *crazy* due to the continued ups and downs in their emotions associated with grief. If a person is prepared for the unique and overwhelming nature of emotions associated with their grief, they can reassure themselves that these are normal and necessary emotions. It is also important to realize that there is not a specific timetable for grief.

Being with others: It is important for a person to be in contact with other supportive individuals. Time together does not necessarily need to be time where grief is discussed. The physical presence of another person is important while a person is grieving. It is helpful to find supportive people that are nonjudgmental and willing to listen when needed. Give clear communication about what is supportive and what is not.

Continue a connection with your loved one: Death may have ended your loved one's life, but it did not end your relationship. It is normal and healthy to continue the bonds with the deceased person. This can be achieved through the use of rituals, talking to them, wearing a linking object (for example: a pin, necklace, bracelet, ring, or earrings), visiting the grave, dreaming of them, continuing to feel their presence in your life, and allowing the relationship to change.

Remember time does not heal grief. A person does not get over their grief. As a person goes through the emotions of grief, the pain will become less intense. However, the deceased person will always be missed and loved.

Exercise: Going outside and exercising at a pace that feels invigorating can be helpful, but do not over do it. Being in nature can be therapeutic.

Plan something to do each day. Despite the pain and low energy involved in grief, it is important to plan something to do each day, even if it is small.

Journal: Write down thoughts and feelings, dreams, experiences, and drawings that are important to release and remember.

Rest: Grieving takes a lot of energy and can affect a person's sleep. It is okay to take naps and lie down as needed.

Purchase something to sleep with. Find an object that is a comfort to cuddle with while you sleep.

Consider a support group. Spend time with others who have had similar experiences and emotions. Groups can be a tool to release emotions, as well as gather ideas about how to cope with the many changes experienced with grief.

Get a pet. If someone feels lonely and likes animals, pets can be therapeutic. Pets provide comfort and affection by their presence and personalities.

Personal possessions: Make decisions about the deceased person's possessions that feel-right to the situation. It is okay to hold onto objects, clothes, and personal items as long as it is helpful. Items can also be donated to family members, friends, or charities when this feels appropriate.

Utilize relaxation techniques. It is important for a person to take care of themselves. A person can use deep breathing, therapeutic massages, or guided imagery to help unwind.

Do what is right and comfortable for you. While there are many suggestions for how to handle grief from others, and education material, it is important for each person to experience and release emotions in a way that feels right for them. As a person experiences their grief, they will find that the emotions and coping mechanisms they experience will continue to change.

Create a memory area. A person can dedicate a part of their home, yard, or other space to the deceased.

Light a candle. Incorporate the deceased into the daily routine by lighting a candle at meal times or keeping a candle lit at the deceased person's usual space.

Music: Listening to and/or creating music can be helpful. Music can be a way to connect with the deceased and your emotions.

Screen your entertainment. Life is filled with many reminders of the loss. When watching television shows or listening to music, the emotions or subjects discussed could evoke emotions in relation to grief. Therefore, it is important to avoid certain entertainment that may not be helpful to you at this time.

Plan ahead for special days. Being prepared for ways to incorporate the deceased and allowing time to experience the emotions of grief can help a person feel ready to face special days. There is no way to predict how the bereaved will react on a special day but having a plan can help to make the emotions seem less overwhelming.

Allow the tears to come. It takes strength to cry. Crying releases stressors internalized in the body. Find a place that is secure to cry and release the emotions. It is important to remember that crying cannot last indefinitely and can be a part of the grieving process.

Education about grief: By gathering information about normal grief reactions and coping ideas, a bereaved person will be reassured that their emotions are necessary and normal.

Complicated/Traumatic Grief

They that love beyond the world cannot be separated by it. Death is but crossing the world, as friends so the seas, they live in one another still.[12]

—William Penn

Complicated grief occurs in approximately 10 to 20 percent of grievers. In the beginning stages of grief, it is normal and expected that emotions may be painful and intense. As a person allows themselves to experience the intensity of their pain, it is anticipated that the emotions will continue to change and become less intense. However, complicated grief occurs when a person continues to feel the intensity of their emotions and becomes stuck in a heightened state of their grief. A person may feel numb and unable to move forward in their life. Complicated grief can include feeling a lack of trust toward others and hopelessness. There may be an intense focus on loved one's belongings and an intense urge to be reconnected with the deceased. It is important to note that these emotions can be common in normal grieving, but they have become intensified and remain as intense in complicated grief. If the pain of the loss is so constant and severe that it keeps you from resuming your life, you may be suffering from complicated grief. Commonly, grievers suffering from complicated grief have some form of negative behaviors or unhealthy coping that develops, and they do not attribute these to the loss or grief, or are even unaware of the negative behaviors.

Some symptoms of complicated grief include (note: these can occur in normal grief too, but in complicated grief they are persistent):

- Intense longing and yearning for the deceased
- Intrusive thoughts or images of your loved one
- Denial of the death or sense of disbelief
- Imagining that your loved one is alive
- Searching for the person in familiar places
- Avoiding things that remind you of your loved one

- Extreme anger or bitterness
- Feeling that life is empty or meaningless
- Difficulty carrying out normal routines or activities of daily living
- Deep, prolonged sadness or nervousness
- Nightmares

Some ramifications associated with complicated grief:

- Post Traumatic Stress Disorder
- Depression
- Anxiety
- Substance abuse/dependence
- Suicidal thoughts
- Chronic impairment in daily living
- Increased physical problems

Types of Unresolved/Complicated Grief

Delayed grief: postponed grief that can last for a lengthy amount of time, even years. For example, pressing responsibilities (settling the estate, funeral/burial arrangements, legal/financial complications).

Absent grief: the griever acts as though nothing happened, shows no feelings of grief, and becomes detached from reality as if the death never occurred.

Conflicted grief: is an exaggeration of one or more common grief reactions due to an ambivalent relationship with the deceased. The person experienced conflicting emotions toward the deceased person when they were alive, and this follows into their grief (love/hate relationships). Some emotions associated with this grief are extreme anger, sadness, and guilt about the turbulent times in the relationship. The bereaved may experience exaggerated anxiety manifested in panic attacks. Substance abuse problems may also arise or existing issues be exacerbated. This type of grief is normally associated with dependent or ambivalent attachment to the deceased.

Inhibited grief: if the griever does not allow themselves to experience the pain of grief directly, they may develop somatic complaints or illness. It can be common for the griever to choose to grieve some aspect of the deceased and not the other—for example, the positive aspects and not the negative ones.

Abbreviated grief: is usually a short lived but normal form of grief. It is often mistaken for complicated grief. The griever has a grief process that is shortened, commonly because the deceased person is immediately replaced (remarrying immediately after the spouse dies) or there was little or no attachment to the deceased.

Unanticipated grief: results from unexpected, sudden death. This can be destructive to the griever and can involve difficulty in accepting the loss; it brings overwhelming feelings. In this case, grief symptoms can continue much longer than normal grief.

Chronic grief: is excessive in duration and does not reach a satisfactory conclusion. There can be normal grief reactions exhibited in the early stages of this grief. However, the grief reactions continue long after the loss has occurred, with little or no progress in the grieving process. They often coincide with an ambivalent or dependent relationship with the deceased, an unwillingness to relinquish from grief, or an intense yearning for the deceased with prolonged intense preoccupation.

In most every form of complicated grief, the griever is trying to deny or avoid aspects of the loss and the full realization of what the loss means to them. It is important to contact a grief counselor, professional therapist, or doctor if you have any of the above symptoms or complications of complicated/traumatic grief.

Call your medical provider or 911 immediately if you have feelings of acting out suicidal or homicidal thoughts.

Coping with Grief on Special Days—Holidays, Anniversaries, Birthdays

You are healed of a suffering only by experiencing it to the full.[13]

—Marcel Proust

After your loved one dies you will be inevitably faced with reminders of your loved one. A sight, sound, place, object, smell, color, song, etc., can suddenly overwhelm you with grief. But this does not mean you will be back to the beginning of your grief. It can be expected that you may experience waves of grief throughout your lifetime and this is a normal part of the grieving process.

Certain reminders of your loved one can be especially difficult on holidays, anniversaries, and other special days. Whether it is the first, the fifth, or the tenth holiday, anniversary, birthday, or other special day, it can be a challenge to make it through the days and sometimes weeks leading up to the date, and then to make it through the day itself. However, there are things you can do that may offer comfort, hope, healing, and growth on one of these special days. Most people will feel better within a week or two after the special day. Over time, the distress of these special days will decrease in both frequency and severity.

Consider trying some of the following suggestions to cope with the reminders and special days that come up:

1. Be prepared. Knowing that you are likely to experience grief reactions when special days come can help you understand them and turn them into opportunities for healing. For example, it is normal to dread or fear the upcoming special day. You may be worried about being overcome by painful memories and emotions, and actually find that you work through more of your grief and find further healing.

2. Make a plan. Making choices for what is comfortable and right for you. Decide what activities you wish to participate in, who you want to be with, and what you want to do on those special days. Communicate choices to others, especially those affected by them, like family and friends. People within the same family can be coping differently and have their own needs. Everyone has their own unique journey with grief. Compromise when possible. Listening and trying to understand each other's needs and feelings, being flexible with each other, talking through each point of view, and meeting each other halfway can be helpful. Including the entire family (children and teens) in the decision-making process about what to do for that special day can help avoid conflicts.

3. Gather with friends and family to recall favorite stories and memories of your loved one.

4. Plan a remembrance ritual, memorial, or celebration of life in honor of your deceased loved one.

5. Find a special way of honoring your deceased loved one. For example:

- Saying a prayer
- Making a toast
- Playing their favorite song
- Making their favorite meal
- Lighting a candle
- Reading a poem
- Planting a tree
- Taking flowers to the gravesite
- Dedicating a plaque or bench
- Planting a flower garden with your loved one's favorite flowers
- Decorating the Christmas tree or filling a stocking with favorite stories or memories and reading them aloud to the whole family
- Keeping old traditions and/or making new ones
- Looking at old pictures
- Making a scrapbook/memory book together
- Doing a balloon or butterfly release together
- Giving a gift or donation in your loved one's name
- Setting a place for your loved one at the table and placing their picture there

- Designing a quilt or expressing yourself through artwork
- Writing letters or journaling
- Making something that symbolically represents your loved one and giving it to family/friends
- Giving family/friends something that belonged to your loved one and may have special meaning for them to have it

6. Listen to your heart and acknowledge limits. Be gentle with yourself. Allow tears to come; allow the laughter and joy. Accept the likelihood that there will be some pain on these special days; give time for it. Feel whatever it is you feel, and express your emotions. It is healthy.

7. Utilize your support systems, for example: family, friends, spiritual leaders, grief counselors, social groups, etc.

8. Do meditation, guided imagery, and other relaxation techniques.

9. Treat /pamper yourself.

10. Look for the joy.

11. Do something for someone else.

Remember, these things may be helpful to one person and not the other. The key is to do what you are comfortable with and what you think might bring you some healing.

References

Kubler-Ross, Elisabeth. *On Death and Dying*. New York, Touchstone Rockefeller Center, 1969

Rando, Therese Ph.D. *Treatment of Complicated Mourning* Research Press, Champaign, IL. 1993

Worden, William. *Grief Counseling and Grief Therapy: A Handbook for the Mental Health Practitioner*, 4th edition, Springer Publishing Company, New York, 2009

Resources for Further Reading

Brener, Anne. Mourning & Mitzvah: *A Guided Imagery for Walking the Mourner's Path Through Grief to Healing*, Jewish Light Publishing, 1993. Exploration of the comfort and ritual of the Jewish experience.

Brothers, Joyce. *Widowed.* New York: Ballantine, 1992. Popular writer shares her personal journey and learnings.

Caine, Lynn. *Being a Widow.* New York: Penguin Books, 1990. Self-help book filled with practical advice and words of wisdom.

Davis, Deborah. *Empty Cradle, Broken Heart: Surviving the Death of Your Baby.* Golden Fulcrum, 1996.

Davidson, Glen. *Understanding Mourning.* Minneapolis: Augsburg, 1984.

Davies, Phyllis. *Grief: Climb Toward Understanding.* Sunnybrook Publishing, 1998. Self-help, poetically written, book sharing the author's experience after the death of her son.

Del Zoppo, Patrick. *Mourning: The Journey from Grief to Healing.* Staten Island: Alba House, 1995. Clinician and bereavement specialist writes from the heart.

Dotterweich, Dotty. *Grieving as a Woman: Moving through Life's Many Losses.* St. Meinrad: Abbey Press, 1998

Feinberg, Linda. *I'm Grieving as Fast as I Can: How Young Widows and Widowers Can Cope and Heal.* New Horizon Press, 1994. Highlights the special circumstances of an untimely death and early grief.

Felber, Marta. *Finding Your Way After Your Spouse Dies.* Notre Dame: Ave Maria Press, 2000.

Grassman, Deborah. *Peace at Last: Stories of Hope and Healing for Veterans and Their Families.* Vandamere Press, 2009. Designed to help caregivers, family members, and veterans understand the impact of war and military culture on lives and emotions. It is a collection of veteran and hospice experiences.

Miller, James E. *What Will Help Me? 12 Things to Remember When You Suffer a Loss.* Fort Wayne: Willowgreen Publishing, 2000. Double book to help bereaved as well as those who want to help.

Miller, James E. and Golden, Thomas R. *When a Man Faces Grief: 12 Practical Ideas to Help You Heal from Loss.* Fort Wayne: Willowgreen Publishing, 1998. Support for grieving men and their caregivers.

Miller, James E. *When Mourning Dawns: Living You Way Fully Through the Seasons of Your Grief.* Fort Wayne: Willowgreen Publishing, 2000. Quotations and support through nature pictures.

Miller, James E. *Winter Grief, Summer Grace: Returning to Life After a Loved One Dies.* Minneapolis: Augsburg, 1995. Inspirational and helpful advice, comparing grief to the seasons of the year.

Neeld, Elizabeth Harper. *Seven Choices.* Centerpoint Press, 1997. Seven-step grieving process as defined from author's experience. May not fit everyone's experience.

Rando, Therese. *How to Go On Living When Someone You Love Dies.* New York: Bantam Books, 1991. Clinical suggestions for a layperson about grief's dynamics.

Ross, E. Betsy. *Life After Suicide.* New York: Insight, 1997. A solid companion for those on this painful and stigmatic journey.

Rothman, Juliet Cassuto. *The Bereaved Parent's Survival Guide.* New York: Continuum, 1997. Covers many important subjects, including particularly difficult issues.

Sanders, Catherine. *Surviving Grief, Learning to Live Again.* John Wiley & Sons, 1992. Information based upon long-term research with bereaved individuals.

Schiff, Harriet. *The Bereaved Parent.* New York: Viking Press, 1978. Practical suggestions written by a bereaved parent.

Schneider, John. *Finding My Way: Healing and Transformation through Loss and Grief.* Seasons Press, 1994. Look at grief as a wholistic process with the opportunity for growth.

Schoeneck, Theresa, editor. *Hope for Bereaved.* Syracuse: Hope for Bereaved, 1995. A collection of short articles on a variety of themes, with many handouts to help grieving individuals.

Smith, Harold Ivan. *Grieving the Death of a Friend.* Minneapolis, Augsburg Fortress,

1996. Helpful look at an often-neglected kind of grief. Walton, Charlie. *When There are No Words: Finding Your Way to Cope with Loss and Grief.* Ventura, CA: Pathfinder Publishing, 1996. Wise, compassionate advice, learned, following the death of his sons.

Additional Resources for Children

Adler, C.S. *Daddy's Climbing Tree.* Clarion Books. 1993. Jessica, eleven, takers her little brother to her grandparent's house to look for Daddy, who was killed by a hit and run driver. She is sure that he is in his favorite climbing tree. The grandparents no longer live there and their dad is not there either. She learns to look for his memory in her heart.

Anderson, Janet S. *The Key into Winter.* Albert Whitman Prairie Books, 1994. Magical story about a household in which there are four keys to open the seasons. A young girl hides the key to winter to prevent her grandmother's approaching death. An allegory for the natural cycles of life and coming to terms with grief and loss and learning to hope.

Beckleman, Laurie. *Grief.* Crestwood House, 1995. A book for adolescents and teenagers dealing with grief.

Bonnett Stein, Sara. *About Dying: An Open Family Book for Parents and Children Together.* Walker and Company, 1974. A book for young children, which is meant to be worked through with their caregiver.

Cazet, Denys. *A Fish in His Pocket.* A boy deals with the accidental death of his fish, which he, without meaning to, helped contribute to.

Clifton, Lucille. *Everett Anderson's Goodbye.* Owlet Book, 1983. Little picture book that goes through the stages of grief in very few words and big pictures.

Cohn, Janice. *I had a Friend Named Peter: Talking to Children about the Death of a Friend.* William Morrow and Company, 1987. After a girl's friend, Peter, is killed by a car, her parents explain what death is and what will happen. School friends make pictures of Peter and decide that as long as they can remember him, he will always be with them in a special way.

Fry, Virginia Lynn. *Part of Me Died Too.* Dutton Children's Books. Children from a year

and a half to eighteen deal with the death of beloved pets, parents, friends, siblings, and other relatives. This book has a lot of stories to tell, each helpful in their own way.

Heckert, Connie. *Dribbles*. Clarion Books, 1994. An old cat comes into a family and later dies. The remaining cats miss the old one and are very sad, but realistic that death is a part of life.

Heegaard, Marge. *When Someone Very Special Dies: Children Learn to Cope with Grief*. Woodland Press. Workbook to be illustrated by the child.

Heegaard, Marge. *When Something Terrible Happens: Children Learn to Cope with Grief*. Woodland Press. Workbook to be illustrated by the child.

Hipp, Earl. *Help for the Hard Times: Getting Through Loss*. Hazeldon, 1995. Self-help workbook for older children, but valuable for younger children as well if only as a source of hints for things that a caregiver could develop on their own.

Krementz, Jill. *How It Feels When a Parent Dies*. Cooperative book for slightly older children.

Kubler-Ross, Elisabeth. *Remember the Secret*. Celestial Arts. A book about death and grief with a more religious background and message.

Mellonie, Bryan & Ingpen, Robert. *Lifetimes: The Beautiful Way to Explain Death to Children*. Batnam Books, 1993. A book about natural lifetimes in all creatures and the fact that sometimes those lives are cut short by accident.

Miles, Miska. *Annie and the Old One*. Little, Brown and Company, 1971. Annie's grandmother has told her Navaho family that she is preparing to die. She will live until the last rug is finished and ask her loved ones which ones they want to keep. Annie chooses her grandmother's weaving stick, but panics at the thought of her death. Although she works on the rug, every night she unravels all the work that is done that day. At last, her grandmother explains that death is a part of the natural cycle, an integral part of creation. Annie understands and begins to weave the rug again.

Ross, Kent & Alice. *The Cemetery Quilt*. Houghton Mifflin. A very wise story of a girl who goes to her grandfather's funeral and talks to her grandmother about death and how she feels about it.

Simon, Norma. *The Saddest Time*. Albert Whitman. Three short stories about different kinds of death and grief. There is an uncle with a terminal illness, a classmate killed in an accident, and a grandparent.

Varley, Susan. *Badger's Parting Gift*. Mulberry Books, 1984. An older badger gives parting gifts to his friends.

Viorst, Judith. *The Tenth Good Thing about Barney*. Aladdin Paperbacks, 1971. A young girl experiences the sad feelings of death in relation to her cat and works through them with the help of her father.

Warfel, Elizabeth Stuart. *The Blue Pearls.* Barefoot Books, 2001. A beautifully- illustrated book written by a mother who lost her adult daughter to cancer. The story relates a dream of angels searching for the blue pearls needed to finish the lovely dress a woman will receive when she arrives in heaven. The woman is granted extra time to love and play with her three daughters while the angel searches for three pearls. A good book to read to young children that allows for an adult caregiver to discuss death from a religious standpoint.

Whitbold, Maureen. *Mending Peter's Heart.* Portunus Publishing, 1995. A boy's dog dies and he is helped through his anger and hurt by his grandfather who describes his own love for his wife and his belief that they will all be reunited in a very good place where there is not any pain.

Wilhelm, Hans. *I'll Always Love You.* Crown Publishers, 1985. A boy's dog dies and the boy realizes that he never stops loving someone even though they have died.

For the Visitors
Guest Sign-in and Special Message

Date:　　　　　Name:　　　　　　　　　Message:

Date:	Name:	Message:

Date:	Name:	Message:

My Life's Reflection

Date:　　　　Name:　　　　　　　Message:

Date: Name: Message:

Date: Name: Message:

Date: Name: Message:

Date: **Name:** **Message:**

Date:　　　　Name:　　　　　　　　Message:

Date: **Name:** **Message:**

Memorial Service/Funeral

Date: _____

Time of Service: _____

Location of Service: _____

_____

_____

Location of Burial: _____

_____

_____

(Obituary): _____

_____

_____

_____

_____

_____

_____

_____

Life Is a Journey

Birth is a beginning
and death a destination
And life a journey;
From childhood to maturity
and youth to age;
From innocence to awareness
and ignorance to knowing;
From foolishness to desecration
and then perhaps to wisdom.
From weakness to strength or
from strength to weakness
and often back again;
From health to sickness
and we pray to health again.
From offense to forgiveness
from loneliness to love
from joy to gratitude
from pain to compassion
from grief to understanding
from fear to faith.
From defeat to defeat to defeat
until looking backwards or ahead.
We see that victory lies not
at some high point along the way
but in having made the journey
step by step
a sacred pilgrimage.
Birth is a beginning
and death a destination.
And life is a journey;
A sacred journey to life everlasting.[14]

—Author Unknown

About the Authors

Samantha Bechtel graduated from Case Western Reserve University, Mandel School of Applied Social Sciences with a Master of Science in Social Administration. Samantha is a Licensed Independent Social Worker with Supervision designation, Certified Grief Counselor, Advanced Certified Hospice and Palliative Social Worker, Certified Trauma Specialist, Certified Ethical Will Facilitator, Certified Guided Imagery Therapist, EMDR trained therapist and a Reiki Master. Samantha has been a social worker for over nineteen years, working in settings such as the emergency room, outpatient mental health, renal care, inpatient mental health and higher education before coming to work with Stein Hospice as a Grief Counselor and is currently the Director of Bereavement and Spiritual Care. Samantha resides in Ohio with her husband and two children.

Alicia Bogard graduated from The Ohio State University with a Master of Social Work degree. Alicia is a Licensed Independent Social Worker, Certified Family Life Educator, Certified Guided Imagery Therapist, EMDR trained therapist, Certified Ethical Will Facilitator and a Reiki Master. Alicia was a Social Service Intervention Specialist with Children Services before coming to work at Stein Hospice as a grief counselor. Alicia resides in Ohio with her husband and three children.

Endnotes

1. www.scrapbook.com>resources>quotes, last accessed May 2012

2. www.quotegarden.com/grief.html, last accessed May 2012

3. www.joyofquotes.com/grief_quotes.html, last accessed May 2012

4. www.quotegarden.com/grief.html, last accessed May 2012

5. www.goodreads.com/author/quotes/28525.Washington_Irving, last accessed May 2012

6. Whitmore Hickman, Martha. Healing After Loss, Daily Meditations for Working Through Grief. Harper Collins Publishers Inc, 1994.

7. www.quotationsbook.com/quote/18772/, last accessed May 2012

8. www.sympathymessages.com/cat/quotes1.htm, last accessed May 2012

9. Keller, Helen. The Story of My Life. Watermill Press, 1993.

10. Miller, James E. When Mourning Dawns, Living Your Way Fully Through the Season's of Your Grief. Willowgreen Publishing, 2000.

11. www.amsa.org/dd/2008/husar%20bereavement%20care.ppt, last accessed May 2012

12. Penn, William. Fruits of Solitude. Vol I, Part 3, The Harvard Classics, New York: P.F. Collier & Son, 1909-1914, bartleby.com, 2001.

13. www.idealquote.com/tag/marcel-proust/, last accessed May 2012

14. www.bellaonline.com/articles/art38718.asp, last accessed May 2012